THE MARTIN FAMILY

Their Secret Legacy

by

Ana Martin & Michele Fischer

Guadalupe Martin at his ranch in Tepátitlan, Jalisco, Mexico

Table of Contents

PROLOGUE

"A Child from the Unknown"

When Ana's father first talked about their family history, there was uproar in the family. Many family members became uneasy about their story ever going public.

The story is that no one knows the lineage of Ana's father's side beyond her great-great grandfather. In fact, they do not even know his real name. Their surname, Martin, was an adopted name for the family.

Ana's family doesn't want people to know their story mainly for fear of ridicule. But one of Ana's brothers says there's something there.

You see, Ana's father's name is Guadalupe Martin. His father's name was Lino (Ana's grandfather). Lino's father's name was Juan (Ana's great-grandfather) and Juan's father (Ana's great-great grandfather) was named Valentin Martin, Jr.…

He was found as a baby in a basket on the side of a wandering horse.

Generations later, the family has slowly begun to reveal that several of them have had many paranormal experiences, many which sound extra-terrestrial in nature. There accounts are genuine and these are very down-to-Earth, sensible, educated people; they are doctors, engineers, accountants, etc. They are merely recounting what they have experienced in their own words.

But with so many unexplained events in several of their lives and the mysterious relative that started their family line, whose origins are unknown, it just makes you wonder…

Could there be a connection?

- Michele Fischer

PART I:

JOSE GUADALUPE MARTIN

Ana's Father

Family Mystery & Unexplained Events

Guadalupe Martin (Ana's father) as a young man

CHAPTER 1

WHO IS VALENTIN MARTIN, JR?

Ana's great-great grandfather

Ana's father's uncle, whose name cannot be recalled, was the eldest living Martin at the time he told Ana's father, Guadalupe Martin, the story of her great-great grandfather.

Born Jose Guadalupe Martin, the great-grandson of Valentin Martin, Jr., Guadalupe is the eldest of his siblings and the only one who knew the story until he told his daughters, Ana and Alicia.   One of Guadalupe's sisters was raised by their mother's family so she never even knew the story of their father's side. They always knew they did not have a lineage on that side but they never knew why. Until he told them on July 16, 2010:

A long time ago in Mexico, sometime around the early to mid-1800's, two horses wandered up to the hacienda of a wealthy man named Valentin Martin Del Campo whose patrolled property ran from Cerro de la Campana to Capilla de Guadalupe in the city of Tepátitlan in the state of Jalisco.

Guadalupe Martin told his family:

"On one occasion, since he had a lot of workers, some of them came and told him, 'Don Valentin, there are two horses (a white horse and a limping horse) over there by the hill of the bell, "cerro de la campana", and you can hear a child crying. They are saddled "encillados".'

And Don Valentin told them, 'A lot of you gather together, surround the horses and bring me the child along with the horses'.

"So they got together and they brought him the child. And it was a child they thought only God knows where the parents were killed. And the child was left with nothing. No family members. Nobody ever found out anything because the parents were never found. No one even knows where the horses came from."

This baby boy grew up to be Ana's great-great grandfather, who was adopted by the owner and also given his name, Valentin Martin Del Campo.

The hacienda owner already had two daughters in their thirties when the infant boy was found that he and his wife would come to raise as their own. Don Valentin Martin was told by officials he had to wait a few weeks before adopting in case the baby's parents showed up. What if the parents had gotten separated from the horses? But no one ever came to claim the baby.

The town's people used to make fun of the mysterious boy, saying he was son of a Russian horse and a limping horse "La llegua Russa y el caballo manco". His self esteem was bruised being called the "son of a horse".

Guadalupe explains: *"Valentin Martin was left with the child and his two daughters who were already older when the child began to grow up. Within time, Don Valentin and his wife died and left behind were the two daughters but they never married. So they became the new owners of the entire capital. In time, the daughters died and the boy, now grown, was left as the new proprietor of all the land."*

Of Ana's great-great grandfather, the mysterious Valentin Martin, Jr., she was told he was extraordinarily handsome and very, very kind. Valentin Martin, Jr. was so good-looking that the wives of the workers would seduce him to impregnate them so they could inherit some of his fortune.

Guadalupe explains: *"All the riches of this land were his but he was already older. The women of the workers were coming onto him and, like a man, he responded. And he started to have children but he gave none of them his own name. They would put the last name of the women's husbands to them. He couldn't give the children his last name because he was single and, like I tell you, he was nothing to the man who picked him up (Don Valentin Martin Del Campo)."* (He was not his real son.)

Ana's aunts and uncles could not remember the name of Valentin Martin, Jr.'s wife. And no one ever found out their mysterious relative's real name or ethnicity.

A possible connection between the unknown infant who began their family lineage to the alleged alien encounters experienced by Ana, her father, several of her siblings and her children was made when Ana met a Mexican psychic in West Covina, CA. The woman psychic, well known in her home city of Tecate for her psychic gifts, was visiting the U.S. for a funeral. Ana asked her for Tarot and palm readings just out of plain curiosity.

Out of nowhere, the woman told Ana that they were descendants of extra-terrestrials on her father's side. Ana at first thought this was absurd.

At this time, Ana already knew the story of her great-great grandfather being found on a horse but never put it together until that day. She had learned the story when she was in high school.

Ana had blond hair since she was a little girl and has light skin, as do all her sisters and brothers which is a common trait in the region of Tepátitlan, Jalisco, Mexico, from which they come from.

But people have always asked her what she was mixed with and she didn't know of anything else. As she and her siblings grew older, their hair darkened. Ana's eyes were light brown (honey color) as a child but also darkened as she got older.

Ana Martin at age 5

The psychic woman even knew that Ana and her siblings were having numerous alien encounters that they kept private and that some of these beings were here to help them and some of them were here to do harm. But she also knew that Ana knew how to protect herself. Ironically, Ana has known since she was a little girl that by Faith she is protected.

"A Divine Man"

Guadalupe Martin (Ana's father) in 2005 with his grandchildren:
Ashley and Aleanna, the baby

CHAPTER 2

GUADALUPE MARTIN

Ana's Father

Ana swears her dad is an alien or a divine force of some kind. ***"There is just something about him that's really different from any man I've ever known,"*** she says.

Guadalupe Martin has never been sick and always has money. Today, he grazes cows and sells them as a hobby. He doesn't worry about never having money; it always comes to him. All that is good seems to come to her father and with ease. And he is always protected. Everyone always wants to serve him in some form or another. He is so humble. A very kind-hearted soul. He's never been a womanizer but always a very loving husband and parent.

He also seems to know things before they happen. He told his one son not to marry his first wife because this, this, and this would happen: same with his youngest daughter, Theresa, about her husband. And everything he predicted happened to them both.

He even told the CEO of a company he worked for that he would die behind his desk watching someone else enjoy the fruits of his labor from Heaven. The CEO broke down into tears because he was ill (which Guadalupe did not know then) and overworked. Sadly, the man died just as Guadalupe Martin said he would.

Driving his young family to Mexico, Guadalupe stopped along the roadside for them to sleep when he shuttered awake from a dream that the road they were on dropped off like a cliff. Cautiously, he drove on and, sure enough, the road was under construction up ahead with a huge drop off that was not marked at all.

What has made Guadalupe Martin, great-grandson to the mysterious Valentin Martin, Jr., so exceptionally protected, fortunate and foreknowing all his life?

THE UNEXPLAINED SCAR THAT DISCHARGED HIM

Take into account the way Guadalupe Martin came to live in America. As a young man, he accompanied a couple of his friends to the Mexican Consulate. His friends had been trying for six months to get approved to live in the United States.

When they got to the line, an official was asking people why they were there to direct them where to go. When they asked Guadalupe Martin, he responded, ***"I'm just here to accompany them."***

The officials told him to wait outside as he was not allowed in therefore. Guadalupe approached a sign that read "Information" and started asking questions about how to go to the U.S. The person told him he could go there on a visa and return when it expired. But Guadalupe said he wanted to apply legally to live in the United States permanently.

So the person asked him if he was willing to join the U.S. military and Guadalupe said "yes".

During initiation into the U.S. military, the troop's "trainer and interpreter" was speaking with faulty Spanish. When the unit commander realized there was something amiss, he asked Guadalupe in front of the trainer, "What's that?" (pointing to his shoes). Guadalupe answered, "Zapatos" and the trainer said, "No! Calcos." And Guadalupe said "NO! "Zapatos". The rest of his troop nodded in confirmation. When Guadalupe continued correcting his incorrect naming of clothing, the interpreter was exposed and arrested for fraud.

When training was finished, the new recruits were sent for their physicals. It was here that a military doctor found two vertical scars on Guadalupe's back: one on his lower back (about an inch-long incision) and another between his shoulder blades (about two inches long). When asked what they were from, Guadalupe explained he only knew about the higher one which was from a cyst that a nun and his mother had removed.

But the lower scar, to this day, he has no idea how he got it. His parents never knew either. And for that reason, he could not serve in the U.S. military. However, he was allowed to stay in the United States or go home. Guadalupe decided to stay.

Ironically, Guadalupe's grown children, his one son and Ana, as well as one of Ana's daughters, all have had probing experiences from unknown visitors and had recurring pain in the same lower back area where Guadalupe's scar is still visible to this day.

The Martin girls at the Martin ranch in Tepátitlan, Jalisco, Mexico, 2004. From right to left: Ana Martin, her daughter Tiffane, Olga Martin (Ana's sister), Krystal (Ana's daughter), Sarah and Samantha(Olga's children).

CHAPTER 3

THE "FAT ROCK" FROM THE SKY

"There were a lot of things that happened that we could never find an explanation to what it was." - Guadalupe Martin

On July 16, 2010 Ana Martin interviewed her father, who speaks Spanish and enough English to get by, with a digital recorder to tell his stories. Witnesses to the interview along with Ana were: Ana's two daughters, her younger sister, Theresa, and her two children as well as Guadalupe's wife, Mercedes Martin.

Guadalupe Martin recounts:

"There are so many stories. When I was young a lot of weird things happened. I'm telling you something like in 1947 there was a place close to us that a huge rock fell from the sky and was the size of a house. And they called it the "fat rock" because nobody ever knew where it came from.

They woke up one morning and the rock was there. It sunk in the earth and a lot of people gathered and started to dig around it. And digging until they managed to loosen it.

The rock ascended to the surface on its own."

Q: Where did this rock come from?

"It came from the sky."

Q: Like a meteorite?

"Could be."

CHAPTER 4

TWIN BALLS OF LIGHT

From the interview with Guadalupe Martin on July 16, 2010:

"Let me tell you what else I did see with my own eyes. On one occasion I saw a light. There were these things they called zorrillas (word for "female skunk"); they were like plants or bushes. Some type of plant with large branches that went upward. They called them zorrillas because they were very strange, weird looking.

On one occasion, coming from my Uncle Valentin's ranch (his dad's brother), I was walking home late at night with my cousin (Rosendo Barba) between twelve and one in the morning. We were walking home that late because we had to wait for the heavy downpour to stop. We walked along the path called "Camino Real" where the donkeys used to pass because there was less water on it.

When we were walking home we started to see a light. There were two lights that were traveling in such a way that they almost appeared to be one; but they were definitely two. They traveled at the same distance. They would go up, over and around these zorrillas. The plants were approximately three meters high.

We stopped in awe to watch them.

These two balls of light, they went up and around one plant and then came down to a certain distance from the plant and then came back up and repeated the same formation around each one of these plants. They did the same ritual to each of these plants and then the balls of light disappeared.

And we never saw what it could have been. We continued walking when suddenly I became frozen in mid-walk.

Then all of a sudden I screamed really loud and my cousin said, *'What happened? Did you fall down?'* I said, *'No, it's next to me!'* And I was paralyzed in mid–motion walking.

He tells me, *'There's no one. Look.'* He started running in a circle around me to show me there was no one there. Yet I could sense that there was something or someone there. And I couldn't move, but not because something was physically binding me. I was just frozen in my walk. I remember even my hands were frozen in mid-air.

How did I regain full body movement? All of a sudden there was a flash of lightning and a loud thunder. When the lightning struck it illuminated the sky in such a way that whatever was binding me loosened its hold on me. And then we heard the splashing of feet running away from us.

Being children, we thought it was another person messing with us. So we yelled after it, *'You son of a - you sure scared us. Yeah, right. Ha-ha-ha'!* We cussed it out but there was nothing there.

The next morning we were telling everybody this story. And no one could say anything. No one had any explanation to what it could have been."

CHAPTER 5

TREASURES FOUND

From the interview with Guadalupe Martin on July 16, 2010:

A BLUE FIRE THAT DID NOT BURN HIM

Once at age 7, Guadalupe was walking a pig home that his father had just purchased. The pig decided to take a nap on the way and little Guadalupe had no choice but to wait for it to wake up. He grabbed a rock and set it against a tree he leaned against to rest himself. Twilight fell upon him when he sees a blue flame come up from the ground in front of him that went back down into the ground quickly. Several times this blue flame shot up from the ground.

Guadalupe gravely put his hand out. The blue flame went through his fingers but did not burn.

A while later, his father found him sitting there. Guadalupe told him that there was fire coming from the ground that did not burn him. His father, Lino Martin, also saw it and said, ***"We're not gonna investigate right now 'cause it's too late and there might be something here that little kids might be frightened of. We'll come back tomorrow."*** He did mean ghosts. They went home.

Next day Guadalupe and his father returned to the spot with a shovel and pick. But by the time they arrived, someone had already dug there. It was a teenager whose mother was having an asthma attack and had sent him out to look for a skunk. At that time, asthma was treated by boiling skunk.

As Guadalupe's family was told by the town's people, the teen had to relieve himself but was on the grounds of someone's property. He did his business by the tree and when he finished, he saw a man riding on a horse he feared might be the owner of the land he just defecated on. So he put the rock, Guadalupe had left against the tree, on the poop to hide it.

When he looked up, the man on the horse had disappeared. The teenager then saw flames come up out of the ground. He dug it up and found a huge pot of gold or silver coins. Guadalupe and his family were told all this later by their neighbors when the story got out since everyone knew everyone.

Prior to the banking system, historically, the Mexican people buried their money in the ground. It thus became a common belief that when a ghost is seen it could indicate money was hidden nearby that must be found in order for the soul to continue to Heaven. But they also believed that if you dug it up, you would die as some did.

The reason for this is metal, especially solid gold or silver, buried for many years creates and traps gases (which may have caused the blue flames Guadalupe saw and explain deaths of people who dug up the buried treasures).

THE BLUE STONE

Guadalupe recalls:

"I was taking care of some cattle as a hired hand for someone else's land and I started to see in a "sanjuan" (dried up riverbed), taller than the tree and deeper still (he was pointing to a fully grown grapefruit tree in Ana's backyard). I see in it something that was shiny. I went to it and started to dig where it was.

I dug approximately three feet. And what do you think I found? I found a little 'cantarito' (a small goblet of clay). I pulled it out and it was completely filled with dirt. I pulled it out. I put a stick through the dirt in it and there was something hard in there. I kept poking but it wouldn't break through. So I broke the cantarito with a rock. Inside it was a stone of a dark bluish color but I can't recall exactly 'cause I didn't pay too much attention to it. I was really small. I was very young, much, much younger than him (he points to Theresa's son who is 8 years old).

It was a colorful stone. It was very shiny. And it was inside of the cantarito when I broke it. And it (the stone) was in the shape of the cantarito."

Q: Like a blue opal?

(He nodded) "I left it there. To me it was ugly 'cause it was just a rock and I didn't care for it. But I do remember that it was very, very smooth. What it was I have no idea."

Interestingly, Guadalupe Martin also recalled an historical trip that may shed some light on the origins of these cantaritos. Around 14 years old, Guadalupe and his cousin Rosendo visited the pyramids in Cacahuamilpa.

"I just remember these pyramids were made by pure rocks (not slabs). I don't know how they did it but this was done when there was nothing but little, indigenous people down there. I know because we saw paintings of these people inside on the rocks.

I remember my cousin and I looking at these paintings where you could clearly see these little people were hiding inside the pyramids from something that was up in the sky. I just don't remember what cause it was so many years ago.

It was a bunch of little pictures of the people with their bows and arrows, pottery…and also, apart from that, little cantaritos (vase shape containers but small like goblets). Like little cups."

CHAPTER 6

AN ENTITY FROM THE FUTURE?

From the interview with Guadalupe Martin on July 16, 2010:

Q: Do you remember the time Grandfather Lino would tell the story how one time he came home drunk and that he went upstairs to get into his room from outside and he saw someone through the keyhole climbing up the stairs?

"Yeah, yeah, he told us that story many, many times. He was mad, intoxicated, and he was arguing with my mother when all of the sudden he saw something and looked through the keyhole (to this day, Mexico still has large keys to open their doors). And something started to come in through the keyhole. He was staring at it and it started to form itself like a person. Lino was yelling at it, *'Yeah, sure, you want to scare me.'* But he was also frozen like me before; he couldn't move his body.

I think it must have been the devil. In forcing itself through the keyhole, it couldn't come in completely so it was forced back out and my father, who was frozen, fainted. This happened when my parents were newlyweds. My dad was so scared he was no longer intoxicated."

Lino had first thought it was a woman but, as it tried to get through the keyhole, he could see it was a man dressed in a 1970's style unfamiliar to him at that time which was before his first son Guadalupe was born in 1931. When it couldn't completely come through the keyhole, it went back out. That's when Lino fainted.

Ana recalls this story because, in the 1970's while watching TV with her grandfather Lino, watching people in "Disco" type clothing, polyester suits, Lino proclaimed, *"I saw that dress code ('vestuario', he termed it). I saw that dress code a long time ago…"* And then he told Ana the story.

What is really puzzling about this account is the fact that this spirit or entity is dressed in clothing Lino could not recognize until some forty years later when the style was worn.

And the impact it made on him. How significantly strange it looked to him in the 1930's, strange enough to make him react when he saw it again in the 1970's.

Be this enigma either ghost or extra-terrestrial in nature, it may be interesting to note here how, with regards to the "Men In Black" phenomenon, people often report seeing men in suits that appear outdated (usually from the past).

CHAPTER 7

ESCAPES FROM DEATH

From the interview with Guadalupe Martin on July 16, 2010:

THE FEVER THAT COULD NOT KILL HIM

"I had to work at a very young age (as young as about 3 years old) because in the long run I was left alone to provide for my siblings, my father and my mother who died at a very young age. She was paralyzed on the right side from a stroke.

So she died very young and my sisters, very tiny, had to learn how to make tortillas and do all the house work.

One day I got so sick, I don't know from what, that I wanted to die.

I don't remember what they called that illness but I do remember that people would be bed-ridden and have a super high fever until they died.

In those days, nobody would survive. As soon as one got this sickness, the relatives would buy a coffin and waited for the person to die. Because no one recuperated. This was during the time when the first highway to Jalisco that passed through Tepátitlan was being built.

There was a doctor appointed for the workers of the highway; they named him "doctor of the highway". That doctor figured out how to cure people from this fever. And he started to cure them.

I was approximately 5 or 6 years old when that fever hit me and, when I was almost dead, I started getting angry (he became tearful even now recalling it). The doctor whose name was Benjamin, but I don't remember his last name, cured me.

And look how many years ago this happened? It was more than 70 years ago and I have never to this day been sick since then. When have you ever seen me sick?"

RIDING THROUGH A DEADLY TORNADO

It was sometime in the 1980's. Ana's parents were driving down to their home in Mexico in a diesel Volkswagen truck. They reached a town in Mexico where they saw people chaining their cars and even big trucks to poles. They drove up to a gas station and Mercedes, Ana's mother, asked the attendant what was going on. He told her, ***"Hurry up and get in a hotel because we have a huge tornado coming our way!"***

But there were no rooms anywhere. Everyone was in shelters not in their homes. They had to hurry up and get out of there because there was nowhere to stay. Speeding down the road, Guadalupe and Mercedes Martin could see the tornado approaching them. They saw cars flip over and a man sitting on top of one car, stupefied, under a bridge. Water flooded into their truck but because it's a diesel it didn't stop. Water came up to their calves inside the car.

The whole time, Mercedes Martin was praying and praying and praying.

Because of the tornado, it was completely dark and a total downpour of rain. They could not see the road in front of them. The tires were barely touching the ground. There was so much water on the road that their little truck swayed like a boat at sea.

Then, in the sky, they saw a cloud in the shape of a dove, lit by the sun behind it. The sunlight pierced through the cloud to the ground. Guadalupe just focused on it and followed it. That's how they got out.

Now behind them, the tornado changed direction.

PART II:

ANA MARTIN

Alien Encounters

Ana and her daughter, Tiffane, 1998, at their home in Los Angeles, CA

CHAPTER 8

BEING WITH THE "ICE CREAM CONE" HEAD

August 26, 2010

They found the dog (which had run out of the bedroom that night) in the bath tub in the morning.

Ana had been abruptly awoken in the middle of the night from deep sleep. Wide awake, she saw a figure floating inside the room, in the doorway. Its head was shaped like an ice cream cone. The head was just below the ceiling, maybe 5 inches. Of the facial features, she can only recall huge freckles, like dark spots, on the face. She does not recall anything about the body. Then she fell deeply asleep again.

Recalling, Ana got the sense that this being was looking for her father who had just left days before with her mother back to Mexico. The being did not seem surprised though that he had gone.

Ana's youngest, teenage daughter, Tiffane, was in a deep sleep when it all happened, "as usual", she claims. Tiffane also reports sometimes waking up in the morning with unexplained bruises on her legs.

CHAPTER 9

SEVERAL ALIEN BEINGS

From the interview with Ana Martin on July 15, 2010 conducted by Michele Fischer:

"This is Ana Martin and I am going to attempt to go back as far as I possibly can. I'm going to start with the most recent. But before I forget, I do want to mention to you that if you go to: www.ghost-mysteries.com/forum/index.php?showtopic=1794 or just Google 'Elathiopia' you will see that I posted something a long time ago that has to do with this experience. Way back then I didn't know what it was.

The latest experience that I had - I can't remember the exact date but it was this year. I woke up in the middle of the night to see what appeared to be – I don't know what it was – didn't know at the time, but after I spoke to someone about it, they said it was called a "Tall White" and it's supposedly a species of alien. And what it looked like was, if you can picture this, if you remember "Gumby & Pokey"? If you can picture Gumby stretched out. Like somebody just grabbed it and stretched it out. Well, it was standing at my doorframe and I could only see as far as where the eyes meet 'cause it was taller than that. It was standing outside my bedroom. So the frame of my door cut off at eyebrow level but I don't recall any eyebrows. But he was taller than that.

Very skinny. And I do remember the hands were very long. I don't recall seeing any knees but if it did have knees it (the arms) would surpass the knees. The face, it's kind of fuzzy to be honest with you, but it's kind of like our features. I can't remember the shape of the head. I mean, no hair, nothing like that. The eyes were big like headlights. I couldn't tell you (the color). This was at nighttime so it wasn't very clear. I never saw pupils on it, not that one or on the smaller versions of aliens that I've seen. Their eyes are dark. No pupil.

He was physically real. He was definitely physically real. The weird thing about it was when I acknowledge that I was actually seeing something…. 'Cause, you know, when you wake up from your dream, sometimes you bring that dream onto your physical plane. So it takes awhile, you know, a couple of seconds, for the body to realize that you're actually seeing what you're seeing, ok?

So when that happened, that's when I realize that I was actually seeing something. I wanted to communicate with it and see what it wanted. At that point, it never fails, I always end up falling asleep. And it's involuntary. It's not like I'm tired or sleepy. I've fought before to stay awake but my eyelids just become really super heavy and I go right back to sleep. That's all I remember on that one."

"The one previous to that was in June; I want to say, 2007. I had spent the night with my daughter, Tiffane, in my brother's home and at that time he was living alone. He had married a gal from China but she wasn't here yet. We had gone over to help him clean and get the home arranged to welcome her into our family. And somewhere around 11 o'clock at night, my daughter, who was 14 at the time, and I, went upstairs to my brother's room. He slept downstairs on the couch in the living room.

Around 11:15, I woke up really frightened, gasping, like when someone rudely awakens you from a deep sleep. I thought that was really weird.

So, dismissing it, I went back to sleep. At 11:30, I woke up again in the same way. And I can tell you the times because he has a digital clock right next to the bed and it's the one that has the big numbers. My heart was palpitating and I didn't know what to think of it.

I thought it was really odd and thought, '*Am I having a panic attack? If I am, why?*' There was no rhyme or reason to it. So I thought, '*Ok, I'm gonna let it go and go back to sleep*'.

The third time I woke up, I woke up because I felt the bed vibrating. And I was wide awake and I thought, '*Hmm, are we having an earthquake?*' And my daughter was fast asleep. She never woke up.

As I laid there awake, trying to make sense of it all, from the foot of my bed I saw a small, what appeared to be, a child-size alien.

And it peaked out and when it saw me, we made eye to eye contact. It immediately, without ever opening its mouth, with thought transference, it told me, *'I'm not going to harm you. I'm just here to observe.'*

At that point, I wanted to communicate with it because I realized this is not the first time I had seen this little one.

I remembered I've seen him before. And when I wanted to communicate with it, my eyelids felt really heavy. And, believe me, I struggled to stay awake. I wanted to talk to him. And next thing, you know what, I fell right back asleep.

Then the next time I woke up, I woke up again because this time I felt something underneath the bed; it was poking at my back from under the mattress. And at that point I had completely forgotten that I had just seen it, minutes before.

I don't know how they do it. But they do make you forget. I had totally forgotten.

So at that point I thought maybe it was a ghost, an entity. I sat up in bed and I yelled out as best that I could, *'In Jesus' name, get out of here, whatever it is that you are. It is not I that commands you but my Lord Jesus Christ. Get out!'*

I quickly woke up my daughter. I said, *'Get up!'* She was half-asleep. We grabbed blankets and pillows and darted downstairs. My brother was snoring the whole time on the living room sofa. We moved the table out of the way. I made our little bed there and we fell asleep.

The minute we laid down, maybe 5 or 10 minutes later, I could feel it staring at us from upstairs. I couldn't see it but I could just feel it staring at us from upstairs as if it were saying, *'Ah, they moved!'*

In the morning, when we woke up, my brother looked at us and said, *'What happened?'* and, jokingly, I told him, *'Dude, you're bed is possessed.'*

And he looked at me and said, *'Did you feel the bed vibrating?'* I said, *'Yes'*. And he said, *'Did you feel someone poking you from under the bed?'* I'm like, *'Yeah, I did!'*

He said, *'It's just my alien friend. He comes from time to time.'* That's when I remembered that I had seen it. Had he not made that comment, I would have never remembered. Never. And that's when we started talking about it.

I said, *'You know, this is really bizarre. It's not something you should take lightly.'*

At that point he said, *'Well, what am I going to do about it, Ana? Who am I going to tell? Who am I going to call? Who am I going to complain to? This is nothing that I have control over and they've been coming to me since I was a kid'."*

FIXING HER BACK

"Oh, I gotta tell you something. When I felt the alien poke through the mattress. The next day, my back hurt really bad. So that night, as I prepared to sleep, I started talking out loud. I was telling it, 'You know what? If you have God's permission to do whatever study you're doing on me that's fine but you gotta fix whatever you put in my back because my back is hurting me'. I felt like I had interrupted what it had been doing to my back and that's why it was hurting me.

That night I fell asleep in the living room and felt the sofa vibrate. Only this time I don't know what happened. I was completely out. But the next morning my back was fine. It didn't hurt anymore.

THE SMALL ALIEN

"This little guy, now keep in mind, if you can picture somebody peaking out through your foot bed, he just peaked out. So I only saw it from the waist up. He had your classic alien look. Exactly what people say that they look like. That's exactly what he looked like. But I do know something for sure, he was not harmful. He had no intentions of harming me at all."

Q: What color was his skin?

"That was like a light grey. It's not exactly a white but not exactly a dark grey either. It's in between the two."

Q: Did he have big eyes?

"Yes, he did. And the fingers were severely long cause I could feel it under the mattress. No ears. And as a matter of fact, I don't remember seeing a mouth or a nose but I know he had them. Totally harmless."

OTHER ALIEN RACES

"This last time my brother and I talked…And the only reason I even know is because a friend of mine - her son is really into this. And I started telling him all these stories. He told me the names and species. So I knew that it was real.

So that's when I told my brother, ***'You are not going nuts. What you're seeing is real.'*** He saw a species which my friend's son said was called 'The Reptilians'.

My brother has seen them in his home. And he's seen the 'Tall Whites' and the 'Greys'. Which again, these names I'm giving you because that's what I was told they were called."

CHAPTER 10

BEING ON "ELATHIOPIA"

"And all we have to do, all we've ever had to do, was get along." - Ana Martin

From the interview with Ana Martin on July 15, 2010:

"I did see one, but I don't know if it counts or not. This one I'm gonna say, like, in 1998 or '99. This was before 2000. This one that I saw was during meditation. But it was also exactly like what I saw in real life at my brother's that night in June. The smaller ones. And this one, I did talk to it and I don't know how I got there. This was when I was experimenting with meditation before I knew what meditation was. I just knew that every time I closed my eyes, but remained awake and shut out the world, something happened.

And this particular time, I remember being in a place that appeared to be gloomy, kinda like overcast. And the floor, I did look at the floor to see what I was stepping on, and it resembled cotton candy. But it was all grey. It was outside.

I stood there and I saw from a distance a bunch of, what appeared to be like, people coming towards me. But when they got closer, I could see that they weren't human; they were all aliens. One of them approached me, and, literally, with never ever opening its mouth it told me, *'Welcome'*.

And I asked him, *'Where am I?'* And he replied, I don't know if he said, *'Elathiopia'* or something to that extent.

I told him that I was looking for God and he told me that I went in the wrong direction. He told me you need to concentrate towards that way. But when he said *'that way'*, when you're up there, there is no left, right, up or down. So I didn't know where he meant to concentrate. I mean, where? You're in the middle of nowhere. Where is 'that way'? He pointed, he was standing to my right, so he pointed to my left. Left up.

He looked exactly like the aliens that we talked about. And was about as tall as me. I'm 5'5". He did look grey, he looked on the lighter shade of grey. Not dark grey but the lighter shade. Nope (no clothes). In fact, the skin resembled dolphin skin. Like dolphin or whale. That type of texture. Of course, I didn't touch it but, you know, from my sight that's what it looked like.
He told me, *'Just be careful'*. He said, *'Because just like on Earth you have good and bad humans. We, too, on Elathiopia, or whatever that's called, also have good and bad.'* But he didn't say 'aliens'; he mentioned another name. And I do not remember because my brain couldn't register what that was.

He said, *'Stay away from the ones that are grey; they are the ones that are against the human race.'* Grey. He did say that very carefully. Grey. I don't know if he meant dark grey, light grey or what. But he just said, *'Stay away from the ones that are grey. They are against the human race.'* And that's when I asked him, *'Why do they want to kill us? Why do they want to get rid of us?'*

And he said, *'Because'* - I'm gonna try to tell you as best that I could - he said, *'Because you humans don't realize the power of your thoughts.'* He said, *'Every single thought that you have goes up into the air. And whether it's a good or bad thought. Anything that's a derivative of one of the two. When it's a bad thought they are like bombs. They go directly up and they disturb where we live'.* And the Greys are sick and tired of moving around.

So the Greys he referred to just want to wipe us out; get rid of us. 'Cause we can't get ourselves together. And the other ones recognize us as being children of God. And, believe it or not, they know who God is. They KNOW who God is. Because he said, *'We recognize that you are children of God, like flowers. We will not allow them to destroy you.'*

So there is this constant battle taking place up there, wherever 'there' is.

And all we have to do, all we've ever had to do, was get along.

Something that, for whatever reason, human beings just can't seem to do. I don't know if it's our ego, our pride. I'm not sure. But the one side is willing to work with us and help us out. The other side says, *'Forget it. Get rid of them. Just get rid of them'.*"

Q: Why do our thoughts have an effect on them?

" 'Cause he said that our mind, our thoughts, they're vibrations. Like sonic. He didn't say these words but I could, as he was explaining it to me, I was seeing it, visualizing it. And do you know, when you look outside it's really, really hot on the bottom of... (like a heat mirage), like flames? Ok, that's what I was seeing when he said that about every single bad thought that we have.

Forget our words. Our words are even worse. Our words are even more powerful than our own thoughts. So everything that has to do with the negativity shoots up like bombs to them. And they're just tired of it. They're sick and tired of it. So there's this battle taking place up there.

I know it's weird. You know what it reminds me of? I'm not a Bible reader but you know where it says we're going to be having wars with principalities and so forth? I know there's something in the Bible that says something to that extent. I wonder if that's what it is.

And without him, him or her. I'm gonna call it a "him" because to me it felt like a male. Although you can't tell if it's male or female. They don't... (have sex organs). I know 'cause I looked. (She laughs)

Well, you know when you realize that you're actually looking at something? I did realize one thing. If you get like excited, like 'I'm seeing something!', they disappear.

If you try to maintain even-mindedness, like, *'Okay, I'm seeing it'* and maintain... There's something about our excitement or fright that makes them go away. They disappear.

Any extreme emotions: fright, anger, excitement makes them go away. If you can maintain even-mindedness. I don't even know how to explain it. If that makes any sense to you. Like a calmness. You can actually talk to them."

Q: Did you get a sense that these beings have emotions?

"Yes, I did. They do definitely have emotions."

Q: And do all these different races live on this one planet?

"No, they can't. I don't believe that they can. We can. We have all sorts of different races but up there they cannot live together. I don't know how I know this but I know this for a fact.

When I was up there and I saw - there must have been hundreds of them wherever this is I was at. I don't know where I was at. I don't know if he said "Elathiopia". My brain registered it as 'Ethiopia' because that's what we know here on Earth. But it wasn't 'Ethiopia'.

But see, when he – how can I explain it – when he was speaking some words to me, because my brain couldn't register it, my brain was seeking other things to connect two and two to what's here on Earth. You know what I mean? Because otherwise I couldn't…"

Q: There was no point of reference.

"Exactly. And this was in the summer when this happened, ok? When I opened my eyes I was freezing. My lips, my teeth were chattering. And this was in the middle of summer. I was literally freezing. It took awhile for my body to come back to regular body temperature."

Ana's elder daughter, Krystal, today

CHAPTER 11

ANA'S DAUGHTER'S EXPERIENCE

Krystal

From the interview with Ana Martin on July 15, 2010:

Q: You were telling me about your daughter and the beam of light through her stomach.

"Oh, yeah, that was a long time ago. That was back in, I want to say in the 90's, like the mid-90's. I woke up. My two daughters and I slept in one bed. And I woke up to a very strange, like a humming noise, 'hum-hum-hum', and when I opened my eyes, I swear to you, I saw what appeared to be a UFO right outside my window, hovering."

Krystal, Tiffane and Ana were sleeping in the far right room of the house in a king size bed. Ana normally slept at the edge of the bed, with Krystal by the wall and Tiffane in the middle. This night Krystal and Ana had switched, with Ana by the wall.

Ana awoke to a very low grade, humming sound that was barely audible. She felt vibration in her body from the humming noise. Her feet by the window, she opened her eyes and saw a UFO outside the window.

"And I remember my daughter, Krystal, was moaning and trying to turn around. She was at the far end of the bed. Next thing I saw was this beam of light coming from the UFO, going through the window and into her stomach.

Of course, being a parent, I went to - and believe me, I was really fighting to stay awake. I reached over my middle daughter that was in between us and I put my hand to block this beam of light that was going into my daughter's stomach. And the next thing I know, I fell asleep. I was out.

In the morning when I woke up, I had forgotten about it. And my daughter kept complaining about a stomach ache.

I made her go to school and they sent her back. She had over a hundred degree fever. She was ill and I couldn't figure out what was wrong with her. Then I remembered that I had seen something outside the window that night and I remembered it going into her stomach.
So I made a doctor appointment for her right away and on our way there, everything went a way. Just like that. En route. Literally, en route. No more fever. No more stomach ache. Nothing. It was gone.

They make you forget and second guess that you dreamt it. Like you're an automaton."

"On another occasion - now this was kind of fuzzy - all I remember is hearing this humming noise outside of my window. The next thing I know, I was running through my hallway trying to hide from this light. And it got me in my hallway, in between the bathroom and my daughter's bedroom. What happened there I don't know. That's all I remember."

Ana's brother has had alien encounters since he (and their other brother) woke with nose bleeds as little boys the year they lived in Tepátitlan, Mexico. Her one brother told their mother that a "little man" put something up his nose.

As an adult, Ana's brother has had many alien encounters, sometimes up to three to four encounters a week. They continue to this day. He wishes to remain anonymous.

CHAPTER 12

ANA'S BROTHER

Ana's brothers (and Mom's sexy legs) in 1965

From the interview with Ana Martin on July 15, 2010:

"I clearly remember when I was approximately 7 years old, 7-8 years old… I was really small and we were living in Mexico. And we only lived in Mexico from, what I can remember, one year. One solid year. 'Cause we've been here all of our life.

One night, we woke up in the morning and my two brothers were covered in blood.

My mom dismissed it thinking they just had nose bleeds 'cause they were bleeding from the nose. And my brother kept telling my mom that a little man put something up their noses and lodged it in between their eyes. Because, back then, we didn't know anything about this. My mom thought he was just dreaming.

But he insisted that a little man or person put something up their nose and lodged it in between their eyes.

Now, ironically, my other brother, he's… I think the reason why my other brother will not agree to any of this or dismisses it is because he's a doctor; so everything in his mind is scientific. There's gotta be a scientific explanation to everything.

But he does remember seeing a UFO at my dad's ranch when we were kids.

My one brother and I sat down to talk one day. He told me that for a good three years he had these encounters 3 to 4 times a week. A week!

To the point, he couldn't handle it anymore. He didn't know what to do. He ended up seeking psychological help wanting to know if it was something he was seeing in his mind or if it was really happening. Until he retaliated and said, 'You know what? No more'.

And he got into, I don't want to say, a fight or a dialogue with them (the aliens). They would call him from downstairs. 'Cause it's a two-story home. And they would wake him up in the middle of the night calling his name. And they would tell him, '*Come here.*' And he would tell them, '*No, you want me, you come here.*' And he would start fighting with them."

Q: You're brother had 3 to 4 encounters a week. What were they doing? Why did they come to him that often?

"You know what, I don't know but he was so disturbed for the longest time. He couldn't handle it anymore.

Now he had originally agreed to have either *UFO Hunters* or yourself set up camp in his home. But last year, his now wife from China, was almost abducted and that is what made him afraid to go forward with it. I mean, think about it.

He told me, *'If they abduct her, how am I going to account for her missing? How am I going to defend myself?'*

But I get the feeling that my brother is being visited by both: both the negative and positive of the alien species. Because why would they try to forcibly abduct my sister-in-law?

Because the one that I saw (the small alien), when he saw me on the bed, he was kind of surprised to see somebody other than my brother. Because my brother had been living there alone for awhile. He was surprised, like, *'Who's this?'* And then he quickly made the relationship, like, *'Ok. They're related.'*

But, yeah, I don't know why they targeted my brother. But they've been following us ever since we were kids. I can remember being as far back as being six, maybe, seven years old and he was frightened of aliens. But he didn't know what they were.

And I do remember waking up and seeing the blood on him and my other brother."

THE REPTILIAN RACE

Q: Have you seen any of the Reptilian?

"No, I don't think I have. But my brother told me one time that he saw all these beings that looked like lizards. He was upstairs and he saw them downstairs. And then we didn't talk about it for a long time."

Q: Did he give any indication that they were human figures with lizard heads or they were all lizard?

"He said that they looked like lizards. They were walking upright like people with arms, legs and a tail. When I mentioned that to my friend's son, he told me that there was a real race, an alien race, called 'Reptilians'. They kind of look like the blue people in the movie "Avatar". Where are they from? I have no idea. They were just downstairs. Moving around. Like searching for something, he said."

Q: Did he indicate that they were good or bad?

"I don't remember. I just remember him saying how they look like lizards."

Q: And the Tall Whites? They're not from "Elathiopia"?

"I don't know where they're from."

CHAPTER 13

HIS WIFE'S NEAR ABDUCTION

From the interview with Ana Martin on July 15, 2010:

"I'll tell you my sister-in-law's experience when they almost abducted her.   Now keep in mind, my brother told us and was very adamant that we not mention anything about aliens or UFO activity to his new wife because he didn't want to frighten her. And we made a pact that we would never say anything about it.

When she came from China, for like the first six months, she kept telling my sisters and I that we have a lot of earthquakes. My sister, Theresa, said, *'Ok, what do you mean, earthquakes?'*

'Yeah, yeah, yeah,' she's said, *'You know, my bed is always shaking.'* Theresa asked her, *'Does it shake during the day or at night?'* To which my sister-in-law replied, *'At night time. I always feel the earthquake.'*

Theresa never believed any of this.   So she questioned my sister-in-law knowing that my sister-in-law knew absolutely nothing about what's been going on in our brother's home. But her responses made Theresa a little fearful and she has never ridiculed us since.

So going back. We didn't want to say anything to our new sister-in-law. We just let it ride until we went to go visit her last year, somewhere around the summer, June-July. My parents always come in the summer from Mexico. That's how I remember dates.

And my brother tells her, *'Honey, tell Ana what happened to you on Wednesday.'* **And she says, 'Wednesday?'** And he said, *'Yeah, remember the E.T.s?'* And she says, *'Oh, yes! Yes!'*

'Cause you see her English was not that good. So she's telling us in her broken English that she was sleeping in the room while my brother was downstairs watching a movie.

Now he was watching a scary movie. And this was late at night. She was upstairs in her room. And she said she was dreaming that there were five E.T.s, that's what she called them, trying to convince her to go with them into the stars.

And she was telling them, *'No, no, thank you. Thank you. I just got married. I like being here.'*

And so they were telling her how this earth was no good. It was very dirty (I don't know what they meant by 'dirty'). And that she should come up there with them. And she kept resisting, saying, *'No, no, no.'* She was really polite; she's a polite girl. She's telling them, *'Oh, no, thank you. No, thank you.'*

She said all of the sudden they turned aggressive.

And each one of them grabbed her by each arm, each leg and the fifth one was trying to choke her as if to make her lose consciousness.

So she started screaming and, at the same time that she was screaming, the girl on TV was screaming. So my brother couldn't differentiate between the two. So he muted the TV to hear what was going on. He heard her screaming and ran upstairs.

When he ran upstairs, she was sitting on the bed with her arms extended. And he said to her, *'Honey, wake up! Wake up!'* He thought that she was dreaming. He said, *'Wake up! You're dreaming.'*

And she said, *'The E.T.s! The E.T.s! They tried to take me! They tried to take me!'* And her arm was stretched out.

The next day, she had a huge bruise on her arm with three prong pokes on it. And they have pictures of this. They took pictures.

And that's when we told my brother, **'You're gonna have to tell her.'** And that's when I told her my experience and what was going on. Now, get this.

CHINESE ORNAMENT TO REPEL ALIENS

The year after that, she went back home to go visit. And she was telling whomever was over there in China what happened. They sent her back with a pouch with stuff inside it, like food, and… you have to see it…a bunch of other stuff.   And this pouch is supposedly to repel aliens. I don't know if it's just coincidence."

Q: It's specifically to repel aliens not just any kind of entity?

"Aliens."

Q: This is in the Chinese culture?

"I guess so. She still has it at home. I don't know if it's worked or not. I haven't asked her."

Q: This could indicate that the Chinese have had alien encounters in their history.

"That's true. I didn't think about that, but, yeah. At this point, human beings trying to explain this to other human beings is impossible. Especially when a lot of people don't believe in this. It's impossible. I wouldn't even have believed in it if I hadn't of seen it and remembered. And it's weird, because once you see it, you start remembering other things. You're like, **'It wasn't a dream; it really happened'**."

CHAPTER 14

ARE THERE ALIEN AGENDAS?

"Human beings have lost the human connection with one another. We've lost compassion for each other. That's what it is. We have lost our humanity." - Ana Martin

EFFECT OF ANA'S "ELATHIOPIA" EXPERIENCE

Q: I'm curious about when you were having that experience where you were on that planet (or place) when you were meditating? From your experiences, what do you think these aliens are up to?

"I think that they're trying to help us. I think that we are destroying our own world, unanimously, everybody. We are inadvertently killing our own planet and they need our planet and they need us."

Q: Why?

"I don't know. Something about the water. But I know that they need us to be here almost as if we were the workers. Like we're the worker bees. Without us, this planet, this Earth, cannot be what it is.

But there's more people being overshadowed by greed and everything else that they're killing the planet just to make a quick buck. Not realizing that we all need it. That's my personal feeling.

And I also get the feeling that this is not the first Earth-like planet that we've been on."

Q: That the human race has been on?

"Right. Because when I was up there, I remember seeing something. This is through my mind. What I'm trying to convey to you is not really simple; because when I was there... I don't know how to explain it. Like it was letting me see other things through..."

Q: Through your mind?

"Yeah. I remember seeing this other planet that was not inhabited by humans but it looks like Earth. It looks like a brand new Earth. Like a virgin Earth. I remember seeing green grass. Just beautiful green grass, waterfalls, trees...

It seems like they're weeding us out. We have too many bad apples. They're trying to help us but those that are stubborn and don't want to get along, don't want to be here for the higher purpose, they're kicking them out."

Q: What do you mean kicking them out. Killing them off?

"Yeah, either killing them off or we're killing ourselves by acting out of greed or selfishness. You know what I mean? People don't care if they step on another, use them, make them go without so long as they get a buck or two. Who cares if the employee goes without?

Human beings have lost the human connection with one another. We've lost compassion for each other. That's what it is. We have lost our humanity.

This was all being conveyed to me through feelings not words. So I am trying my best to put it all into words. But words do it no justice.

You know what, the more we talk, the more I remember little things that I had forgotten.

They really have our best interest at heart but we are our worst enemies. We are our own worst enemies. And it's all through that little ego - 'I want more. I want more. And I don't care if you have less!' And not giving a damn about other people that are starving in this world. Other people that don't have what we have. You know? Oh, gosh, it's really awful."

Q: The ones that are evil, is there any reason why they haven't just obliterated the whole planet?

"They're trying to."

Q: How are they trying to?

"They want to just do (away) with us all. The others are trying to save us. And the way that they're trying to is to get through to our own heads. And I'll tell you how. I'm going to try to explain to you as best as how I understood it.

If you take a person and tell this person over and over again, they're no good, they're no good… eventually they'll believe it. And then, no matter how much someone else tries to tell the person, 'You're good', it's already in bred within them. They won't listen to you. So they become a slave of their own mind. They become your slave."

Q: So a lot of our thoughts may not even be our own?

"That's right. Oh, gosh, you said that perfectly. When you think about this, since you were very tiny, your thoughts have never been your own. Your beliefs have never been your own. They've been the beliefs of your ancestors, your immediate family, your church, etc.

If you get a parent that raises a child to believe this color black is actually white, no person on the face of this Earth is gonna make that child believe differently later. This is how they do it."

Q: Now what about the good ones? What do they do?

"The good ones are trying their best. You know where the word "faith" comes in is what they're trying to work off of. They're trying to let the others know that we can better ourselves; we can better the Earth. This Earth doesn't have to cease to exist.

But we gotta stop killing it. We have to stop hurting the Earth. We have to stop hurting each other.

And it all starts with being of assistance, being of service, to your own human race.

Q: Did they give you any indication… do you get any sense from them about the future?

"The future has yet to be written but I feel like we are winning. The good side is winning."

Q: Did they say anything about 2012? About December 21, 2012?

"No, I haven't talked to them in awhile since that one contact that I had with them. But, as far as 2012 is concerned, I know that a lot of people say there's going to be solar flares and blah, blah, blah. I don't think so. But don't quote me on that because I don't know for sure.

I think 2012 marks a point as to where our next step is going to be. Are we going to finally say, *'Ok, enough is enough. Make everybody equal. Help everybody?'* **Because in helping out others we also help ourselves.**

Or are we going to let the human race continue fighting and killing each other? 'Cause that's what's gonna happen if we don't stop it. And it's all through desperation. If you don't have any money, how are you going to buy your food? Anyway you can. Whatever it takes to feed your family, that's what is going to end up happening.

And you don't need an alien to figure that out for you."

EPILOGUE

"My Own Experience at Ana Martin's House"

After having been talking to Ana as a friend for almost a year and recently spending a full weekend with her and her daughters, I have found Ana and her close-knit family to be very grounded, sensible and genuine people who love life and who could not be more "real" and down-to-Earth.

This is the first time that they have ventured to go public with their personal experiences and their family secret that they have kept very private for all of their lives. And they do so with reserve and caution.

Yet even spending my first night in Ana's house, I had my own personal experience with the unexplained. Sleeping in the living room, I woke up in the middle of the night and right beside me on the couch, a little above me in mid-air, I saw a transparent, pixilated ball of light of an emerald green. It had a center circle that seemed to be looking at me, if I remember correctly. Whatever it was, was gentle; it did not frighten or alarm me. Then, slowly, it drifted back away from me, almost like lint in the air. And vanished.

I took it as a "waking dream" I sometimes have where I will see something very random and out of the ordinary (and usually transparent) for only a brief moment when I first open my eyes.

It did not appear to be real but…can I really be sure?

Perhaps one day, the Martins will be able to learn the meaning of these continual encounters they have with the unknown.

Perhaps one day, evidence will appear that will shed more light on what happened that brought those two stray horses with the mysterious baby who would grow up to be Ana's great-great grandfather. Evidence of who he really was and where he truly came from.

Another thought: if Valentin Martin, Jr. indeed fathered many children prior to his own family, how many other families could there be today who have his genes and may perhaps be having extraordinary experiences that they can't explain?

- Michele Fischer

Visit:

martinfamilybooks.com

for further details about "The Martin Family: Their Secret Legacy",
its authors and future books to come.

Ana Martin is currently working on her next book that will dig deeper
into her and her family's extra-terrestrial and paranormal experiences
that continue to occur to this day.

<u>ORDER ANA'S HOMEMADE SOAP BARS!</u>

This unique soap is made of only all natural ingredients that Ana received through her daily
meditation, specially combined to restore all skin types to their natural state of pure balance
and radiance.   Ana's relatives of all ages, from infant to elderly, benefit from her safe and
pure natural soap.

Order Ana's "channeled ingredients" soap through her website: ***martinfamilybooks.com***

For interviews and appearances or to reach
Ana Martin or Michele Fischer directly, contact:

anaandmichele@yahoo.com